# Spring in Grandma's Garden

Bo Penny

# Spring in Grandma's Garden

Story by Bo Penny
Illustrated by Olena Kiptelaya
Edited by Ivana Jenkins

To my dear Malina, and to all children
who love nature and playing in the garden

As the sun peeked through the curtains of Malina's room, a robin landed on her windowsill, chirping joyfully.

Malina sat up and rubbed her eyes as she woke to the sound of his morning melody. Suddenly, she jumped out of bed, "Spring is here!" Malina exclaimed as she ran off to find grandma.

Malina was very excited because grandma had been preparing the garden for spring and she promised to let Malina plant some seeds this morning. Malina loved grandma's garden and couldn't wait to get started.
"What can I help you plant first?" Malina asked.

"Hold on a minute" said grandma.

"Gardening is hard work!
First we should have a nice,
healthy breakfast so we don't
run out of energy."

Malina could hardly contain her excitement.

She gobbled up her breakfast,
brushed her teeth,
and ran for the door!

"Oh but look! There's something special waiting for you by the front door!"

Grandma had a surprise.

A brand new pair of yellow rubber boots and yellow garden gloves to match, and a straw hat with daisies tucked in the band.

"Oh I love it grandma, it looks just like yours!" Malina exclaimed as she showed off her new hat.

"There's one more thing we need to do before we go outside." Grandma declared. "We must protect our skin from the sun's rays."

Malina reluctantly stood still while grandma put sunscreen on their faces, arms, and legs. Now they were finally ready to work outside.

Everything around them was bright and cheery.

Birds and bees were singing and buzzing and greeting them playfully.

Snowdrops and yellow daffodils nodded their heads as if to say "Hello! What a beautiful day!"

As they crossed the yard Malina saw bunnies nibbling on the bright green grass.

She even spotted a groundhog peeking his head out of a nearby burrow.

"Today we will plant peas and lettuce." Grandma said.
"But first let's see if anything new has sprouted in the garden."

They opened the gate and right away Malina could see
bright green stalks poking out of the soil.

"What are these, grandma?" Malina asked.

"Those are onions that we planted last fall." Said grandma. "Look how much they've grown already!"

"Now let's put on our garden gloves and plant some peas!" said grandma.

With a small hoe, grandma made shallow trenches and Malina carefully dropped the seeds in one at a time. She then gently covered them with soil.

Once the peas were planted
they did the same for the lettuce.

And before they knew it
they were all done!

"When can we eat the peas and lettuce, grandma?" asked Malina.

"Well" said grandma "we'll have to come back next week to water them and weed them so they can grow better. If we take good care of them, we can harvest and eat fresh lettuce and peas in just a few weeks.

Happy with the work they'd done, Malina and grandma closed the garden gate and headed back to the house.

Suddenly, Malina had
an idea - mommy loves flowers!

"Grandma, can I pick some flowers
for mommy, please?"
asked Malina.

"Of course!"
grandma replied.

And off Malina went
to pick the biggest and brightest
daffodils for her mom.

"Here comes your mommy now!"
Grandma exclaimed.

Malina ran to show mommy
the flowers she picked.

She couldn't wait to see the look
on mommy's face when she
gave her these beautiful daffodils.

"Mommy, I helped grandma plant
peas and lettuce today.
Can I come back next week to
weed and water them so they can
grow better?" Malina asked.

"Of course, that sounds like
a wonderful idea."
Said Malina's mom.

"Now say goodbye to grandma,
it's time to go home."

Malina waved to grandma.

"I love you grandma.
I'll be back to help you again next week!"
she said.

As they parted ways, Malina smiled and said

"What a wonderful day we had
in grandma's garden!"